DAYWORK

DAYWORK

poems

JESSICA FISHER

MILKWEED EDITIONS

Published 2024 by Milkweed Editions
Printed in the United States of America
Cover design by Mary Austin Speaker
Cover art: *Flora Stabiae,* photographed by Marco Pedicini
Author photo by Beowulf Sheehan
24 25 26 27 28   5 4 3 2 1
First Edition

Library of Congress Cataloging-in-Publication Data
Names: Fisher, Jessica, author.
Title: Daywork : poems / Jessica Fisher.
Description: First edition. | Minneapolis, Minnesota : Milkweed Editions,
2024. | Summary: "A meditation on art's longevity and the brevity of
human life from the highly acclaimed, award-winning author of
"Frail-Craft" and "Inmost.""-- Provided by publisher.
Identifiers: LCCN 2023028850 (print) | LCCN 2023028851 (ebook) | ISBN
9781639550722 (paperback) | ISBN 9781639550739 (ebook)
Subjects: LCGFT: Poetry.
Classification: LCC PS3606.I7755 D39 2024 (print) | LCC PS3606.I7755
(ebook) | DDC 811/.6--dc23/eng/20230626
LC record available at https://lccn.loc.gov/2023028850
LC ebook record available at https://lccn.loc.gov/2023028851

Milkweed Editions is committed to ecological stewardship. We strive to align our
book production practices with this principle, and to reduce the impact of our
operations in the environment. We are a member of the Green Press Initiative, a
nonprofit coalition of publishers, manufacturers, and authors working to protect
the world's endangered forests and conserve natural resources. *Daywork* was
printed on acid-free 30% postconsumer-waste paper by Versa Press.

for Louise Glück, in memory,
and for Margaret Ronda

> One law of fate requires that people
> Should know each other, so that when
> Silence returns, there will also be a language.
>
> FRIEDRICH HÖLDERLIN

CONTENTS

And when you are ready, take some of the aforesaid lime mortar, well worked over with spade and trowel, successively, so that it seems like an ointment. Then consider in your own mind how much work you can do in a day.

CENNINO CENNINI,
Il libro dell'arte, c. 1400

DAYWORK

SHADOW PLAY

Autumn. Light. Under what
sun were you born, did you grow.
Under what king, what tyrant.

What window. What door. The four
horsemen, the seven sisters, at rest.
Whether a thousand years, five thousand,

is a long time. Still, a stone
held in the hand will warm.
The same goes for bone.

Who fed you, a hand extending
the spoon. What fed you, music,
art, or light. Was there an empty room,

shadows cast upon the floor,
the boards liquid with sunshine,
and was that how you imagined

the soul: open, ready, very still,
even if the day itself was windy.
Or was it for you like the wind,

tempestuous, infiltrative,
lifting the fallen leaves.
Did you think about it at all.

Many lights cast many shadows,
so that the hand on the paper
is reflected time and again,

the knuckles like the mountains,
one range after the next, and each
a fainter version of the same color,

so that our sense of the faraway
is brought close, the brush dipped
again into the water, a little less paint

for the next stroke. The path
curving away to the right, around
the hillock, into the copse.

A little gate breaks the view.
Beyond, the beyond,
given as a stripe of blue.

This is how I came to know you,
as a smudge or trace—thumbprint
on the potsherd, residue in the flask.

1

HINGE

When I was a child, I was given a coin, caked in dirt. Tell me, she said, from whence came this coin, and whom did it serve, its mint or its king. Served in a cake, or for a cake, was it traded?

So I was ushered into the corrosive questions, each one hinged, as if there might be some movement, a door shut then opened, and behind the knob, the agent of change. But either the screws came loose, and the door fell askew, the tongue flapping free, or the hinge had rusted shut, and I was dumbfounded. In either case, it was I who had broken what I should have opened, as if a bull in a shop or led to the slaughter. Come along, pretty heifer, said the priest who held me, and when I tried to speak, I heard the bellowing.

Who pities the beast, its eyes wide and wild, that braces for death, and hopes to be changed? Three wishes she gave me, and along with them the stories of those who had squandered their wishes by wishing. Scattered to the winds, and the fourth wind left hungry; still it sweeps past my door, crying mine, mine.

CAMERA OBSCURA

In the darkened schoolroom decades ago,
he lit a single candle, and through a pinprick
in the board he held up to block the light,
it cast its flame on the wall. We were to draw
conclusions from what we saw, map
the geometry through which the flame
might pass without heat, as abstraction,
through the cardboard lens. We took out
our rulers, our colored pens, and began
to draw. It was very cold in the room
and our breath showed in clouds
in the little bit of light the candle gave;
outside the playground lay gray and empty.
I was still deciding how to spell the words
for which there are options, gray or grey.
I followed the others, took on one friend's gait,
the way another one stood waiting. It was
a practice of thought. We knew from our lessons
that each experience was to lead to a new proposition,
written out longhand as hypothesis or proof.
I got caught up in the phrasings of speculation and
certainty, in the tone of it. When we traced the flame
in our lined notebooks there was no way to
indicate that it was alive, hot. We drew it
as you might an almond standing on end.
When we were done he told us to put our things
away in the zippered pouches, told us

to close our eyes. That the darkened room was
inside, the pinprick inside: this is the proof, he said.
And that whatever we saw, had seen, or would see,
the world we thought home, passed through the eye.

PEAL

Because the child is slight, and new to his task, it sounds like a halfhearted attempt, though from the way he ran from the barnyard to the chapel, taking the four steps two at a time, it seemed that he hoped to make the bell ring loudly, to make it peal, as one might say, with joy. But it's a small bell, and he still a small child. No one will hear this ringing, tinny and private, and so his grandfather follows behind to show him how to throw his body into the task, riding the rope downward and letting it jerk back free, again and again. Since it isn't meant to tell the hour, he rings it at will, thirty or forty times. When he tires, the clapper does not strike but rather rolls around the rim, as a dog in need of water lets his tongue loll.

This is the world now, the chained dog lunging to bark around the corner, vines growing through a broken window. What was it then, when the chapel was new, its hewn rock altar dragged into place, the walls skimmed with slaked lime. Not a question exactly, but still I would like to know. Time the essence, then as now, pigment seeping into the wet plaster, the day's work marked out in advance, therefore each segment of the fresco called a day. Christ in a bath, his wounds raw, and below him the mother and child, and saints to her right and left. Elsewhere bits of color uncovered from beneath the whitewash, in patches a few centimeters long—blood dripping from a foot, and across the chapel a few squares of an interlocking design. What you see is never the whole story, of course.

If this were another time, a dog barking, fruit hanging heavy on some tree, a pregnant woman walking uphill slowly as the bell rings the town to rosary—if this were now, time as it has always been—but something changes even still, though I can see what they saw and feel what they must have felt. This was their one town, they were born in it or came across the mountains on foot or horseback, fearing something or wanting something. Stones laid together made a town, high above the other towns. They built a castle; the neighboring town, a tower. Who could say which was better? Winter fell heavily on both, the snow in drifts against the stone walls, heavy on the tiled roofs, the tiles often falling with the load. Because the damage was inevitable, they left a hole in the roof through which the snow fell, an unblinking eye, as if held open for irrigation. A ladder through the hole, to repair the damage when spring came.

ORIGIN

Who shelters from the storm, beneath the covers or in the mountain cave, cannot but be assailed by the wind, the sound of it penetrating even here. I had a penny to wish upon, a doll with cornsilk hair, a sister and a brother to call my own. To make a bride, you must open the doll—the doll must open. They would show you how. The squirrel in the winter pines traces the shape of a V, down one branch, up the next, from tree to tree, never meeting the ground. The poet too must move that way, from thing to thing, where the branches cross. In the show of the master draftsman, there was a study for the hand whose touch was the first touch. Necks craning in the crowd, to see what he had made. Let me show you, I said to my children, the birth of the world. Let me see.

DAYWORK

Close your eyes, he said, and took my hand.
There was something he wanted to show me:
the seam called the *giornata*, raised like a scar,
running through the fresco, which marks
where one day's work ended, the next began.
I wanted to trace that limit, to know
where the painter had found an edge
and stopped, the scaffolding descended
and the brushes washed, the figure left to dry

in the dark room, his one eye painted open
that will never see the rearing horse he rides—
you know the posture, you've leaned back in the saddle,
the beast beneath, you pulled at its reins
and told it to quit. It can't quit, the bit in the mouth
and no sight in its eyes, seen and yet blind.
This was the drama he wanted to show, don't you think,
or think of the women holding the room up,
the stonelike caryatids with their gray, empty eyes—

have you ever felt like that, like you are to keep
very still while the others move around you?
In birth I remember the midwife took my reins,
is that right, she held me here and there and reached
inside, she was touching my baby, I had nothing to do
but let it happen, I let it happen, so well trained really,

a vehicle, you ride me or drive me, oh but if you are
the head I am the neck, I will turn you to my advantage,
will make you see what is wrought through me—

IN THE DREAM

we rode in a chariot through the roiling ocean,
    a team of four horses pawing the water,
    urged onward by someone—
        he lashed them ever deeper with his long whip

wondered when I woke *why*, my eye as if pierced by a sliver
of that mirror I read about as a child, that would foul all you see
the way the black spots spoil the silver, the rose,

    the rubble of empire seed for a new city, a city of ruin,
    the carved figures fading through the centuries of rain,

      record of what sacrifice, of what dominion—
    the Dacians with their hands tied,
        or Pluto's thumb dimpling her thigh—

as I write this, my daughter wakes, crying Mama! Mama!
why do they wake with fear from sleep, what darkness is inside

it was the quiet, she says, it wasn't the dream but the quiet
when I woke, the dream was beautiful, you and I hiked
to an abandoned cottage, the washing was still on the line,
you could pick up little bits out from the ruin, the wildflowers
were as high as my thigh, isn't that wonderful

should I sleep again I think that I should sleep again

LYRIC

I dreamt you were sad, L having left your daughter for another woman; we watched as they walked through the new exhibit on the technologies of light, their movements projected in a flickering loop over the old film reels. And there was a hidden chamber, like a storeroom, with a panel that opened when pressed, filled with things that didn't fit into the gallery, little mock-ups of girls in short dresses and long beads, 1920s or '60s I couldn't tell. The things in that room, though beautiful, weren't needed or weren't wanted, and your sorrow was there, like a kaleidoscope, only made of sound.

Was there something I could bring you I asked, and you said no and then yes, since your husband was away, walking the hillside or sitting at the café still, looking through illustrated pages cut from the book of children's verses, whispering *This is the truth*—

Since you were very hungry, but for what you couldn't decide. You were distracted by the sound coming from your throat, a low hum, like a refrigerator, like a grasshopper who has made it until winter, rubbing his frozen wings. Done for.

And in the gallery the new couple was dancing, though the celluloid had caught fire in the projector, a black hole blooming through the image, while the curators hurried to salvage the last of the scrolls to be found, a long poem on paper, which would, we all knew, be lost if the flames came that far—

DAYBOOK

1

My pretty new book marred
and some sort of ruin

I wrote down what she'd seen
and it was ugly

the door ajar
and Jill forced down on her back—

2

I tried to paint the stain out
but the ink bled through

and now the page is a blue smear
rough to the touch

On the reverse my daughter
has made the world

In it a bird flies by
its wings a hurried scribble

on the carefully drawn body
A burrow shaped like a boot

opens underground
There's a rabbit like a cat

with a heart on its head
& diamond buttons

on the girl's boots
on her bodice and crown

So you see once again
violence is to beauty

as the warp to the weft
always somewhere beneath

3

(At Pompeii)

The brothel is narrow
and the visitors enter

a few at a time, stare at Priapus
with his club for a cock

as they file into the rooms
with the small beds of stone

where lay the daughter
of Salvius, Nike

from Crete, Panta,
Beronice, Restituta, Mola,

Cressa, Victoria,
Marca, Fortuna, and Myrtis

4

Unwound cassette ribboning the asphalt, its shiny spill
And whatever voice, and the body it carried, overrun

The pages of the book printed double and so torn from the spine
And sound on the ground, the unspooled pool of tape

Doubled or doubled over this forced union an undoing
If the body then hers, if not the body then whose

What violence begets more violence and voice
It unravels in the cold air, is carried somewhere

Aegina Alcmena Ama Amanat
Amare Amina Antiope Asterie

PALEOGRAPHY

text to Text whose weaving
    who is weaving
pretty girl little spinner
    hope the warp the weft
the shuttle the rod
    in the room a little sex
a little credit a scholar a lover
    hate mail or fan
a sympathetic book a basic fact
    how to recover the dead
(her middle name instead)
    (her maiden name)
against my better judgment
    I decided to put them to rest
concerned why the punch line
    why am I obsessed
(her maidenhead) (the erstwhile dead)

THE SLAUGHTER OF THE INNOCENTS, 1376
(Capitoline Museums, Rome)

Above the worm-eaten wood at the bottom of the panel
a woman kneels in black, what child laid to rest there
where the paint has long since worn away—

The children have discovered now
in which corner of the museum you are hiding
and want to see what you see,

Look, you say, lifting the smaller
to show him the baby nursing,
the hooded nursemaid drawing a bath,

so as to draw his gaze away
from the lure of carnage—

*

Why is this the scene that holds your attention,
figure upon figure in the shallow foreground
as if players on a stage: the soldier with his sword

drawn, the mother lifting her infant son
to the point. It was so early, then,
there was so much the artist couldn't manage—

lines of perspective, transparency of a tear,
what violence is, what grief, how it contorts
the body. Somehow the failure of it

compounds the pity—having struggled a long time
to get things right, the poems of that winter
so leaden, so dead. Another day of heavy rain,

we rode the #42 down the hill to the center,
to the museum, the boys on our laps,
not so long since they were inside—

*

They liked the Colossal hand, the twins
suckling the wolf, the bronze horseman;
were hungry, drank the blood-orange juice

as we looked out over the city—what to do
with so much beauty, you can't really take it in.
So strange, then, to be caught up in this

world of grief a few millimeters thick,
prone to loss by flood or fire or the slow wear
of time, paint flaking from the surface,

the wood pest-tunneled. Still, it makes it worse,
somehow, *not* to believe, the fiction so thin,
and still to feel. For what? There's nothing there.

*

The baby on my hip is tired, his friend
bored. We turn and go, but I still can't shake
the thought of him, whoever he was,

painting with a single gesture
murderer and the bereaved mother
bent over the place her son must have lain,

their same set mouths and the isosceles
of their eyes, and the arms that reach
toward absence, how to show it,

the innocent wood underneath,
the innocent ground—

the woodworm's erasure so complete
they might as well be planting a field
together, tamping the soil down.

MORALITY PLAY
(December 18, 2012, Rome)

Because you've said *I can't imagine it*—the sword parting
the child's head from his body, caught in the act—there's
something cold in the room when you do. A shiver through
the museum, the waxed wood floors and pale gray walls, the
unobtrusive lights, all part of the ploy in which the eye is
force-fed. The image there even after, as you watch them on
stage, in the school play. *Condolences for your country*, from
the mothers who embrace you as you wait in the lobby of the
theater for the doors to open. And then by chance twenty on
the stage for the finale: the exact number. Yours is a flower
in her makeshift costume and sings her sad song: *I would
that I were seen.* The unexpected violet forcing itself through
the snowdrift, its sweet scent remarked on in the song they
sing together, as the thought of violence forces itself through.
Whose red heart blooms through her coat. Must this once again
be my subject.

TRIPTYCH

Left the children screaming at the window
    Deaf to their language, their cry like the seagulls'

Entirely separate, and in what medium
    The children flank the portrait, as decoration

So too the woman with her stone gown blown behind

SPOLIA

On the inventory of stolen items,
cycad, sondergast, bitter orange, Emily.

Fruitlessness, inyourface, driven on, suffocate.
Or instead, taken to bed.

The unopened book full of answers,
until open. Then questions.

Then foxglove for forget-me-not—
something to stop the heart, nostalgia's antidote.

How many hours spent in those rooms,
empty of us now. There was nothing

to salvage, so we went out back.
A certain order to destruction there,

a cycle to it. No, it didn't make it easier.
Wanted to drink until drunk,

make an imprint. Not lasting—
like a sock. A little drunk, the shape

of your head on the pillow, seam
of the pillow lining your cheek:

2

PARABLE

From the highway, we saw the mountains. We didn't need a map to tell us what they were called, their peaks jagged as teeth in a sunken face. Between incisors was a castle, just perched there.

Because it was not yet midday, we decided to stop. We passed through a few towns before the paved road gave way to dirt; eventually that too came to an end. We parked by a high wall cloaked in passionflower and, hungry, stole some of its fruit. You said, *Come along, my princess*, tucking a blossom behind my ear.

We thought the wall would hide our theft, but a man was just opening the gate. *Come inside*, he said, *they are better with wine.* We followed him to the kitchen, where there was a table already set with glasses. A small sharp knife with the imprint of the *abeille* lay on its side. He pried my hand open and took from it the damaged fruit. From my hair, the flower, which he set before me.

Read it, he said, *so that I may read you.* It was, I knew, a story of the Passion, though I did not remember who played all the parts in that gruesome tale. My tongue lay still in my mouth, while the knife in his hands made quick work of dissecting the fruit, which in the end was filled with the larvae of bees. *What have you suffered?* he asked, taking my hand.

I did not want him to spread my palm open, to bring the light closer, any more than I wanted to find myself in the scene I once saw: in a rough-hewn farmhouse kitchen, a knife like his slipped while cutting a girl's hair, and, slitting her brow, freed the spiders nesting there. She was a reader by trade and she knew what they spelled, their black bodies arranged like type on the white of a page.

I have lived in this house when the water ran and when it ran dry, he said, by which he meant someday soon someone would find him. Neighbors in the valley brought by what they grew: there would be a basket of produce carried away, a bottle saved for the wake. We do know, after all, what the future holds.

But you are also a host, a runaway bird, he said, pouring the wine. We drank in silence, too startled to answer, and followed again as he stood from the table and led us out into sunlight. We thanked him and turned, glad to be out of that strangest of houses. I wanted to run but knew he was watching, had seen me already a long time ago. So I just took your hand, trying to seem casual, and walked on past where the road met its end.

The ascent to the castle was steep and rocky, but finally its walls rose from the outcropping. In parts now broken, still it stood against the sky, its little windows cut out as with scissors. The doors were blocked, so you hoisted me up to the lowest window, then found a foothold and followed me in.

The castle, it seemed, was already well discovered: on makeshift tables we found hundreds of boxes, each marked on its side with the name of the kind of thing that had been pulled out of the rubble. Coins of gold, silver chain, bits of iron, leaden bullets. One table for metal, one for bone, of oxen and fowl, and digits arranged in a box by finger, and bits of skull with their dentelated edges. Human, mind you. *Someone lived inside this room*, you said, peering through the eye sockets—

and then swept it all aside, the bones of the past, trinkets of the dead, to clear a place for us to lie. Bridegroom, here is my body. Through my hair, your fingers.

HIVE

In their darkened cells, locked in
with wax, the larval bodies hardening.
Are they scared in there, the children
want to know, does it hurt to change?
In the dark room, in the sealed cell.
How am I to know? When I think of their hive
I think of her lungs, honeycombed by illness.
That was the word she used for it, long ago.
Since in a net I seek to hold the wind,
Wyatt wrote, meaning he could not.

SPEEDWELL

The sun goes down, we say,
but that's not right. Still, night falls
on the tragedy's final act.
The first star like a pinprick in tin.

I was looking for a metaphor.
For someone who knows the way.
On the shelf a book titled *The Sight of Death*.
On the shelf a little bottle to keep age away.

How can you be alive you growths of spring?
Whitman wonders, fed by death,
in the poem my friend loves.
The field itself, some kind of bed.

For what sleep. She wrote to say
that this spring may be her last.
I lay on the damp earth, in the grass
interwoven with the dozens of plants

I'd thought nameless, the little white
daisylike flowers and the tendrils
of the tiny striated blue ones,
which have, as it happens,

not only the one name *speedwell*
but many more besides, *bird's eye*,

cat's eye, farewell and *goodbye.*
You were to pin a posy of it

onto the beloved's coat
before a journey, the boat leaving
for what distant shore. The passengers
reluctant to go, as is the poem

that knows it has to come to an end
and refuses, like a child stalling
before bed, not tired yet or scared
of the dark. Every death takes

a body; it's hard to know what it leaves.
Already it has stitched its signature
into her chest, the scars that chart
her illness like lines on a map

that show where the ship has sailed,
struck rock, found the ocean too deep
to anchor and so drifted windless,
the sea, like the earth, teeming

with the dead. And from those graves,
these flowers, which every spring
have bloomed, discrete as the beloved,
and if we are to believe Whitman,

and why not, *of* the beloved as well,
hair or tongue or the unseeing eyes

that were the color of chestnuts
and are no more. Why not lie

in the grass in the sun, taking
the flowers as proof that nothing dies.
This is what the poem's after,
after all: a figure, no matter how thin,

that might make these reversals
in matter seem like a switch flipped on
and off, off and on. A child playing
day and night, dark and light.

A single life like that, or not at all.
If in the bag the phone rings
and goes unanswered: will she
feel like that, calling from far away.

RAPT

Through the long shadows, parrots,
like the last green leaves, take flight,
their call across the grass. The pomegranate
on the leafless tree pecked open,
a gash in the ruddy side.

Too thin for winter, its cold will burn her.
Whether she married in joy—
something thin about it now.
The child flinches when she leans in
to kiss him, sometimes she is

a bird pecking at the last sweet kernel,
sometimes an arrow shot clean from the bow.
Whatever is felt, covered over in cloud,
nine oktas wide, as if in fog or falling snow.

THE VOICE

Voice kept coming in and out

the connection got bad
when I moved toward the couch

went back to the window
where the signal was stronger

looked out onto the brick wall
soon to be demolished

tried to imagine what the space
will be once it's gone

could think only of an absence of brick
and not even that really

Only the problem was on her end
Impossible to catch what she was saying

It does that she said when she returned
meaning the phone

and then I lost her again
and the conversation still going

I mean we weren't done talking

NATIVE

left out   overnight
the cry   like a cawing
a voice   calling
at the edge   of the meadow
the uncultivated   ditch
narrow   as a grave
we lay there   in rain
the weeds   above us
native   to this

THE MATCH GIRL

I read somewhere, years ago, of a girl with matches in her apron pocket or tucked into her petticoats. I can no longer remember what the story was, whether a fairy tale or fable, or why it mattered that she should carry the promise of fire, of a hearth warmed or a forest burned to ash. I am sure I had not thought of her until last night, though in that cabinet of the mind she must have remained, waiting. She knelt in a clearing, sheltering a flame. The ground, covered with the yellowed needles of the pines, was a tinderbox, and throughout the surrounding forest were patches of fire, the trees orange and crimson, the sky very still and the gray of cooled lead.

When I woke I wanted to tell you, because she had your eyes, and wore in her hair the gold pin that was yours, when you were alive. There are certain illuminated books that have been unopened for a hundred years or more, on the shelves in the great libraries or lost in some box, and in their pages sometimes people wait, in the ornate initials or peeking out from the windows that frame them. How can you not imagine them oppressed by the closeness of the codex, wanting air, light? I have never been able to shake this ridiculous fantasy, that they are real, as you are real still, and the scribe who traced their features, and the apprentice who pricked and ruled the page, and the tanner who scraped the skin, and even the calf with its wild sad eyes, whose veins still ghost the vellum. And so she seems to me, that girl in the dream forest, who surely meant something when she came to me, though she didn't see me standing there, did not look up from the flame.

DARK CRYPTIC
(after Louise Nevelson)

I was a child,
night a black box.
I lay in that
narrow bed
as the darkness
took shape
around me
and so I thought,
what cannot
be touched
is real.
I didn't feel
myself to be
a weight,
didn't know
the gravity
that kept me there
as the lid closed.
Nothing said,
there is
form within.

IL VIAGGIATORE

After the opening, there was a dinner.
Children in the garden, the sound of water,
gravel underfoot. The painter's husband
sat beside the poet at the long table,
inclining his dark head toward the older man.

You would have said the latter was closer
to death. And so he was, a little,
though the theme of the evening
was the deathlessness of art, the ancient
stories once more transformed—

*

The last weeks of spring, days lengthening,
the shadows reined. And then an end to it:
the sticky heat, a desiccated frog under the swings
in the park where their children played
as they took down the show. After spring

came summer: the banalities of time, unchanging.
The children's hair, bleached in the sun, salt-
thickened. The coarse world, noisy, full of places to go.
Bodies in water, breaking the medium, or flung
out in sleep on summer's borrowed bed.

*

August claimed the older man; the patch
of stubble that was hard for him to shave,
was shaved. The other shook sand
from the bedding, the towels, folded
his legs under the steering wheel of the tiny car,

red or blue I can't remember, left the expanse
of sky and roaring water to return to the city
which had by then made its point,
light returning after dark to the night-chilled
statues, antiquity's stone *alive*—

*

Fall to winter, a litany of days. Here,
snow and then thaw, the sycamore's
white bark against the blanched sky.
And in the midst of this evenness, news

of death in midlife: a blind spot
in the field of vision where the beloved fell
away, leaving a wound like wing marks
in the snow that show where death
descended, in the shape of a bird of prey.

NEW YEAR

A mean dog chained
Frost in the grass
Had to keep moving
Went the wrong way

One side a meadow
Full of sharp stover
The other, the river
Where ice had bent
Reeds to the water
The stalks staked down

Saw that and more
Tracks and the tracked
In winter at daybreak
Stood standing there waiting
The blue sky cold

What for, you asked
Not really a question
Or was it the wind
High and lonesome
I took you for

EARLY SPRING

Today a veil of mist drawn
over the mountain,
the mothers pushing their
strollers down the path.

On the table, a mirror, window
to the sky. A surface through
which time moves, but there is
no record.

       All the while—
a shadowy underworld.
A world between us.

That we didn't know it to be
like the rime ice on the grass,
the first flower pushing
through the weight of snow.

See this, see this:
the only manual, for how
to get through.

And the dream, dissipating
now, in which I followed
a river that dried into
bracken, that gave way

to a dream of you
touching me, as if
no time had ever passed,

and every touch shifted
something, the way
turning a kaleidoscope
alters the view. Gone now,

though sleep like snow
is absorbed into the body,
and changes it.

3

DEAR FRIEND

1   April 4, 2019

There was a meeting in the morning
presided over by a bottle of juice no one drank
then time to prepare for the next thing
in between I walked under the sky
pigeons landed on the building's narrow beam
then tried to land elsewhere
they are back now it is time to nest
the crew was out cleaning windows
suspended on their orange lift
livid, *nitid*, a word I didn't learn until later that day
I watched as they maneuvered their machine
remembered sitting in the borrowed office that first year
I was talking to Hillary, looking through the grimy window
when suddenly a man hovered there
we spoke in code through the glass
as he washed the window clean
the mind goes down these little warrens
sometimes memory sometimes obsession
a student for example wrote of kids neatly wrapped
in their neat blankets, and the abyss opened
what is *neat* I wondered where does it come from
I followed one thing to the next it led me there to *net*
from *nitid*, from *nitere* to shine
such light through the glass
where did the time go all the neat things we saw

the word was my father's it belongs in my mind to him
to all that he was taught
to clean with fury to praise the small things
neat did it neatly now I am crying this poem doesn't want
to consider the father's coming blindness the dark world
widening in his failing eye *this is the day* he would say
when he woke me *rejoice and be glad in it*

There was champagne at the afternoon meeting
but no celebration and at dinner after the reading
the panic again I wanted you there
everyone had been to the conference we didn't attend
twenty-five thousand cramming the planes the Ubers and Lyfts
eating and drinking, edibles and karaoke, for poetry
no one wants a Cassandra at their table but what the fuck
we live in time this time of suffering
trace of this present in future time
drove a friend home down the rutted road drove home
through the fog wondering where do they go when they go
your mother our friend do you remember
the night we slept in the tent under the starless sky
the sound of the waves incessant something always going on
too soon it will be someone else's turn my father's for example
does he really believe in the soul and what is it
he thinks about when he thinks about it
no one cleans their own windows
he would say as he got down to work, leaving always
the glass of those he loved transparent as water
the Windex-soaked newspapers balled up
and whatever news the days gone by had held
smeared into nothing—

In the ocean, what might you find? This is a prompt for the child too nervous to write, for the mother who feels at day's end that she has seen it all. And the essay still unfinished, which was to be so easy. The mind moves, but to what pattern? And that whale road we saw, crisscrossed by the mother with the notched tail, the baby with the white spot in the shape of a frigate bird. We ran starboard to port to follow them, before the boat turned—are they somewhere still crossing? Where are you? In an earlier time, evening still ahead of you. Citrus in the garden, and rose. And the child at school or just home, and the work done or almost done or not yet begun. Once I saw a school of flying fish leaping free of the water, and once a flock of birds that turned and wheeled in the hot October air, above the fresh grave, as if to give comfort, serving so readily as metaphor for the soul. Their wings disappeared in the bright sky, then flashed black and white, then disappeared again, some sort of text emerging and fading. Since I am a teacher, and the papers are due tomorrow, I know there are dozens of rooms in which someone works or ought to be working; they feel their minds move or they don't give a damn. I want it to matter that we were here at the same time, late capital postindustrial my sweet aunt with her one good eye my sweet friend who called as I was driving home. As always, we talked of poetry, what it is for, and the lonely tired night was full. Why do I tell you what you already know?

3 March 6, 2020

It already seems a long time ago since we stood in the rubble where the fill juts into the bay. Someday in the future I will think back to us then, how we saw where sea touched earth; salt, sand. A way of framing things—I know that. Ever since the first class in college, where we cut a rectangular hole out of a sheet of cardboard, and she said, to be an artist is to select. She said to impose the frame on what we saw, so that it might become art, which means that what I was taught is that art excludes. I miss you. I see that through the frame. But I am torn now, writing this, between things: a book about the past lies open beside me, marking one writer's fascination with lives seen only through the shadows; beneath this document other windows are open, one to the article on the spreading virus and one to the *Decameron*, which I have been meaning to read, and one to the grant application that would give me time to write. I am like a dragonfly, flitting. Like a fly landing here and there. I miss you. I am not at a precipice, nowhere near the sea; but grief is a watery thing, not mine thank god at the moment, though still it meets the ground and undermines the shoreline. My father just now on the phone, saying that after his friend had died, his heart hurt. I didn't know in which way he meant. My heart hurt, he said, missing her, and the doctor I know, and who knows me, said he felt that way when his wife died, and it was in fact his heart that was hurt. But she was only a friend, my father says. The doctor said he should have a stress test, only they aren't really very reliable, they can say there is a problem when there is not one and they can say there is no problem when there is one. And so the doctor who recommended a stress test said,

Only if it still hurts when you've been walking on an incline. My father prefers the neighborhoods, which are flat, and meandering because they are built along a cliff, and therefore the edge they encounter cannot be subsumed to a grid. He likes to come to the view. But because he needs to know why his heart hurts, whether from illness or grief, he says he will walk the canyon or certain streets in the neighborhood that head uphill. He will not come to see us, because his heart might be fragile now or might be in the future, and at his age—well, he doesn't take it for granted anymore. And I thought then of you, the way your heart hurt, the speed at which it felt to be beating, and how, when they hooked you up to see what it was, they found it was just what it is to be alive now.

There is the stumbling sound of a hurry now as the girls— my daughter and her friends—rush downstairs. They are fascinated with murder. Jughead dead, but not dead, he faked his own demise so the preppies wouldn't kill him, is basically how it goes. And when they are taught consent, they tell me, laughing as I show them how to peel garlic, they are taught to order pizza, are you hungry and how do you like it, which means that their love will be in language from the beginning. Will be about knowing. I didn't know how to speak when I first was touched—it was electric, I was a current. Something like that. Thinking this—but they descend, want the couch where I am sitting, writing you. The oven timer has been beeping a long time, but I don't want to give them the couch, don't want to go turn off the timer. I want to remember that I was like a wire once, conductive, mute; desire surged through me. Want to be that wire. What are you doing, they ask, and I say, I am trying to write everything. Iris has squeezed in beside Sylvie, then Mira and Erin, on the couch; on the loveseat are Phoebe and Grace, looking a little left out. *It does not say RSVP on the Statue of Liberty.* They are watching *Clueless.* I saw it with Esther, or with Lara, when it was just out. Before I had become a conduit. When we thought the future would be a screen, and would remember what you had in your closet. Where are they now. "Lara would be an asset to any team!" the website assures, but Esther is lost to me, though I remember everything about her, her middle and last names, her aunt Kashia and her fake British accent and each long afternoon we spent in her rambling house, watching *Inspector Gadget* or flipping through porn in her closet. She wanted everything, had to choose.

It's cool to know what is going on in the world, the brother says in the film, so I turn back to the paper. "The Only Choice Is to Wait for Death," one headline reads, "along roadsides and in olive groves." Now the car lights bend around the driveway's curve, and Dylan is home from the basketball game in the town beyond the neighboring town. He is ravenous, a warrior returned from the field. When he has gorged himself, and the bones are left scattered about his plate, he turns to what he must become, Macduff to some Macbeth, in the fourth-grade play. That great bond which makes crow to wing. Meanwhile, someone has matched the CDC guidelines on how to wash your hands to Lady Macbeth's "Out . . . out"—

4   June 17, 2021

I am looking out the window onto the patio where once we dragged the folding crib, put the boys inside to play. Trace of you here, trace of your voice in my ear. I used to wonder how it is that it happens, bodies that once lived inside coming to stretch their lengthening legs in the sun, knees grass-stained. Or that you are no longer just there beside me, bent over a book or writing something in your loose hand, paring fruit or letting the sand fall through. Not a rift—just, you who were so close, are farther now. Attention widens, takes in more of the world, until it reaches where you are. Mind like the pond: something touches the surface, and the ripples form. *Lots of motion in the sky and ocean all the time*, you wrote, when the snow fell around me, the fields a canvas for shadow. Searched again to find what time it is there, what season—you are now always a little ahead. The moon, we share, slivered or gravid. How can it be that she is steady, though steadily changing? I imagined her pulling the earth as a child does a toy, a dark thread linking her to us, tying her to our tides. And so I was not surprised to see the linea nigra emerge as if from the umbilicus, from the water body inside. I remember the rain fell as your contractions came, that you were very quiet in pain. Memory is just another thread, unraveling. There's so much I don't recall, time frayed or unwoven, though I can still see the soles of your feet as they were that day, the child's eyes opening when he was mostly still inside. None of this is for the history books. But I think of the artist who, when commissioned to make a memorial to the war dead of her hometown, turned instead to the living. There was a story from that place of a girl saved by a blue ribbon, which appeared from nowhere, carried by the wind, and led her out of the mountain cave, where the shepherds sheltered, as it collapsed. How to follow its lead? The artist asked her townspeople to help her tear ribbons from bolts of blue fabric, and bind each house together, and then to the mountain. In the film of that day, you can see the women in their black skirts and kerchiefs rolling the strips of cloth, twenty-seven kilometers altogether, on the sunbaked square, the children dancing giddily down the narrow streets, their arms filled with the tangled skeins. Between balconies and windows they tossed the bundles until the town was stitched together by a thread the color of the sky. So it is that love, too, distinguishes a crucial archive.

NIGHT SONG

You'll never know
what became of me
in the dark, how
my body opened, to
what or to whom.
There, the moon
shone with the sun's
reflected light
and the stars, hidden
by day, blinked their
shy hellos. The long
days of summer, with
its great foliage, its
flocks and herds,
had erased the desire
to be a self alone.
Sometimes on the bus
I felt like a stowaway
in other lives,
looking into the soul
of each passenger.
How, you ask? given that
the soul, if it exists,
cannot be seen, is
like the bird hidden
in the bush, the
air you breathe. You

take it in nevertheless.
I studied their hands,
the laborers headed home,
kids on their way
out for the night. Beneath
the skin, the riverways
that lead to the heart.
I caught their eyes,
held them there awhile.
There was no one
I could not love.
When the wind clattered
through the oak trees,
and the last milkweed
seeds clung to the
wire screen, and the
crickets sang their wild
song at nightfall, I
thought everything was
saying goodbye, that I
should listen more closely.
I wanted to throw
the window open
to that cold, take in
whatever was left outside.
The leaves of the aspen
already so few, though
they are not lonely,
and in the ravine
a net stretched wide
to catch the saw-whet

owls in their migration.
There in the moonlight
I saw one shining,
lured to the snare
by its own call
played back. Later,
under black light, I felt
the rapid heart beating
in my hands, spread
a wing to tell its age,
the dun feathers fluorescing
the color of sunrise
or sunset, the breast
soft as milkweed tufts.
Weighed and banded and
then let go, it flew back
into its anonymous life.
It had survived capture,
was ready to hunt.
The night was dark
as the future, and
very cold. It drove
us inside, but something
stayed with us of
that strange kind,
their eyes like citrine,
their few ounces
nonetheless weight enough
to hold a heart.

ROUNDABOUT

Brought a cup of water
Showered again

There was a problem of litter
Whose bandage there

You were driving through the city
I was supposed to navigate

The app said we were nearing the Pantheon
But we found just another roundabout

Someone there was headed against traffic
You swerved to avoid collision

Around the fountain in the center, picnickers
Why call them that, that's not what they were

A woman lying there rose to vomit again
Where were we heading

Writing this, I see it now clearly
The theme *strung out*

Someone studying
Why times were hard

I brought him water in a paper cup
Too full to hold its shape

We were there for a meeting
Whose bandage was time

AFTER EMPIRE

Passing on the right
The swerving truck at Cerveteri
At the end of empire's drunken reach
In the sea

Past the Etruscan wells
Wide as a body's span
Hand over hand, legs spread

And the river the breadth
Of a little boat paddling hard

Red hill cut open
Clothed in green

Nothing to make of it
But you could watch it all day

This river narrower than the last
This one a stream
The next almost dry in the summer heat
This stream wider than the one before
The next a river running like a train on its burnished track

The rivulets within her aging hands
The skin thinned

Always somewhere a crossing
The bridge we walked through the shaggy wind
The stone whipped clean by it
Her bright eyes watering

Someone strong enough
To row against the current
Or carried away past knowing

Wanted to move like that
From one thing to the next
To write without thought
A passenger merely

Past the white throat of Carrara's mines
Containers stacked into a Rubik's
At the turnoff to Parma

On the far side of the 12
Vineyards terraced into the mountains
All made to satiate some hunger

Salt on the skin from within
Or close now to the ocean

Only so much description can do

The mountains too high
For our hands to have touched

No
Nothing we haven't touched
And around us the ruins

I thought of Michelangelo finding a fault
In the nearly finished stone
It couldn't be done

But where work ends the work begins
Sign of that hand on the marble still
Sign of that eye

Into the tunnel here we go
Beauty has an end
Where it ends something opens

What to call it, memory
The long tunnel, feeling of breathlessness

On the other side, a forest in which
Something must live unseen

Pebbles just visible in the river's curve
The highway snaking over it
Its bridges and outwashes

It leaves a bar, an island in the center of it now
No child would draw it like this
The wash of rocks on either side of the summer river
The eroded earth, trees piled at the banks

And no love like the love of profit
That's what you wanted me to believe

How to prove otherwise

The hill above the tunnel was lit and blooming
And something must live there
Where our hunger is fed, if hunger is fed

SUNSET CORNER
(after Helen Frankenthaler)

Rust spreads, there is a seam,
green coming through again,

a single line makes the horizon,
past which we cannot see—

instead we watched the surface
where waves spread, clouds

casting their shadows, a silver stretch
where wind riffled the still water—

against that, what thought?

No thought, the movement
of not thinking—slurry of sand

falling through fingers onto the fortress
the child builds close to the break,

bits of cobalt and bottle-green glass
jeweling the ochre expanse,

its towers rising and falling,
and above what substance,

air as the voice is an air,
in and out of the bodies it moves,

into the "crooks and fools in power,"
the songbirds and sycophants,

children running ahead, and the mind
borne forth that way, to no end—

THRALL

1

If vibrant, if a little older now, if homesick or homebound, if original, if originary instead or in a cloud, if whatnot, if rupture, if seam or seamless,

if the other closer now, the earbuds the sparkling band, the intrigue of privacy, if vegan or virgin, if bearded and pierced, if pierced and shaved, if razed,

if sorrow buckles the body as heat buckles steel, if the fifth floor collapses onto the fourth, if undone, the rift opening within, if the pen gripped in the hand or the hand loose as the tongue, the subject an object suddenly, the matter of it,

as if the edge of a pink bra showing, a nipple held high as if to mean fullness, if hungry and then full, the other inside, if the other inside, as flesh and symptom, if the pleasure of watching, the power to continue, without knowing, unknown—

if the other beloved, the transient ridden or the sliver untoward, if honey not butter, if butter not egg, if egg not fish, if fish not flesh, if the cage is safer, if safety in numbers, if the state unthinkable, the state of affairs—

2

If there was a memory that unchanged alters, sand and the
sea or the wind-funneled avenue, as at the heart of a pearl,
some irritation,

if the shape of a rose, accidental, ocular, if the philosopher's
eye, unlike any other,

if push and then shove, the music beginning, if *e* not *a*, if *j*
before *e*, if the other's beloved, if he's gone by the way,

if violence a mother of beauty's bounty, the layered nacre
iridescent as the caustic clouds of polar winter,

if earnest and hungry, the right hand pouring, and the thin
stream of milk seems light's very source,

if seeking or forsaken, the language unflowered, lifted and
tossed as leaves in a squall,

if desire undid the shape of your seeing, the feeling unbidden,
the book almost ended,

could it be there could be, if another mind greater, a thought
for that field each separate blade blowing—

3

If you're borne forth on rhythm, the body now tired, the other another, the shirtsleeves unfurled,

broken down on the parkway, hungry, belated, the car overheated, the cottonwood drifting,

if the young have more fun, if young love was sweeter, if hunger's insatiable, if the bright orange means danger,

if each to her own, if the children are grown,

if the words grow strange in my mouth, a crypt in my knowing—

is that the subject again now, the shadow premonitory, that rides once again beneath the penman's right hand, hides itself in the ink of the nib—

4

Will I return then to wander the texture of nighttime, the
red lines on menus the orange bars on roadblocks,

to wonder, how will we mourn the mother, under what omen,
a flag or a sign, the mean wind blowing,

and again the strange thought, where does it come from, that
stitched to your breast was a ribbon of satin—

hunger undoes us we've known it we know it, clatter of
silverware rattle of thought, the sound of the feet clicking
on pavement,

a rhythm I like, what is it, strange birdie, its calling in
springtime—

a wait undid me, someone is wanting, I know that there's
time, a time of frustration,

hustle me hard, the music a burden,

in the mania of night the color of bottles the flatness of
painting sharp cry of children the sound that defines me no
such promise time's sleeping

LISTEN

The page as the sea, or the sea a page on which what is written
will be read only in this instant—

so many dark nights, the line of waves breaking again and again,
so many times when even you who were there looked away.

Listen now. My voice, if it is a voice to you, rendered or carried
here, comes as surely someone has come to you, mother or
lover,

someone shouting through the break of the waves, under the
cloud-filled sky, on the beach that was as dark as inside,

no light on the water, no substance to the sound. So it was
when you listened through sleep to the voices heard through
wall or door,

when the door opened and the beloved lay beside you and
spoke, though you were asleep, and did not hear.

NOTES

"Origin" describes visiting the special exhibition of Michelangelo's drawings at the Metropolitan Museum of Art in 2018.

I wrote "Daywork" after visiting Raphael's Room of Heliodorus in the Vatican Museum with one of the conservators responsible for its restoration.

The first section of "Daybook" rewrites a line from W. H. Auden's "As I Walked Out One Evening"; there, he describes a world where "the Giant is enchanting to Jack, / And the Lily-white Boy is a Roarer, / And Jill goes down on her back."

In "Morality Play," the line "Whose red heart blooms through her coat" is taken from Sylvia Plath's "Poppies in October." The Italian mothers' condolences are in reference to the Sandy Hook massacre on December 14, 2012.

"Hive," "Speedwell," "Rapt," and "The Voice" are for Hillary Gravendyk, in memory.

In "Hive," the line "Since in a net I seek to hold the wind" is from Sir Thomas Wyatt's "Whoso List to Hunt."

"Speedwell" takes its question "How can you be alive you growths of spring?" from Walt Whitman's "This Compost."

"Dark Cryptic" takes its title from Louise Nevelson's eponymous sculpture.

"Il Viaggiatore" is in memory of Seamus Heaney and Bruno Boschin.

"After Empire" refers to the sculpture Michelangelo began for his own tomb, which he abandoned due to finding faults in the stone.

"Sunset Corner" takes its title from the eponymous painting by Helen Frankenthaler. The phrase "crooks and fools in power" is taken from Michael Palmer's "Scale."

"Dear Friend" is for Margaret Ronda and represents my side of an ongoing correspondence. The poem's third section quotes the 1995 movie *Clueless* and a *New York Times* article on the war in Syria titled "'The Only Choice Is to Wait for Death.'" The poem's final section describes Maria Lai's *Legarsi alla montagna* (To bind oneself to the mountain), her 1981 collective performance in Ulassai, Sardinia, which extended over three days and involved almost all of the town's thousand residents.

ACKNOWLEDGMENTS

Many thanks to the editors of the following publications, where some of these poems first appeared: *The Believer*, *Beloit Poetry Journal*, the *Bennington Review*, *The Equalizer*, *Hampden-Sydney Poetry Review*, *Poem-a-Day*, *Poetry Daily*, *Poetry Northwest*, *Tin House*, and the *Yale Review*.

This book was born out of the year I spent in Rome as recipient of the Joseph Brodsky Rome Prize, awarded by Drue Heinz Trust/American Academy of Arts and Letters. Fellowships from the Hellman Foundation and the Oakley Center at Williams College assisted in the completion of this manuscript. I am grateful to these institutions, and to Milkweed Editions, for their support.

With gratitude to the wonderful community of artists and scholars at the American Academy of Rome for the experiences and conversations that have sustained me this past decade. Thanks, too, to my brilliant colleagues and students, who continue to inspire me.

Deepest thanks to this book's first readers, including Ann Fisher-Wirth, Camille Guthrie, Robert Hass, Stefania Heim, Fady Joudah, Anita Sokolsky, Roberto Tejada, and Emily Vasiliauskas, who each helped me better see a shape in its kaleidoscope of concerns, and whose encouragement gave me the patience to keep turning the lens. Thanks especially to the late Louise Glück and to Margaret Ronda, both brilliant editors, who read the book in its various iterations and tirelessly worked through every line. The grief of losing Hillary Gravendyk is at this book's center; I remain grateful for her poems and friendship.

Heartfelt thanks to my friends and extended family for their love and support. And, as always, to Dan, Sylvie, and Dylan, who show me every day that love writes its own history.

JESSICA FISHER is the author of three collections of poems, including *Frail-Craft*, which won the 2006 Yale Younger Poets prize, and *Inmost*, which was awarded the 2011 Nightboat Poetry Prize. Her honors include the 2013 Rome Prize, a Holloway Postdoctoral Fellowship in Poetry and Poetics, and a research grant from the Hellman Foundation. She is an associate professor of English at Williams College, and she lives with her family in Western Massachusetts.

milkweed
EDITIONS

Founded as a nonprofit organization in 1980, Milkweed
Editions is an independent publisher. Our mission is to
identify, nurture, and publish transformative literature, and
build an engaged community around it.

Milkweed Editions is based in Bde Óta Othúŋwe
(Minneapolis) within Mni Sota Makhóčhe, the traditional
homeland of the Dakhóta people. Residing here since
time immemorial, Dakhóta people still call Mni Sota
Makhóčhe home, with four federally recognized Dakhóta
nations and many more Dakhóta people residing in what
is now the state of Minnesota. Due to continued legacies
of colonization, genocide, and forced removal, generations
of Dakhóta people remain disenfranchised from their
traditional homeland. Presently, Mni Sota Makhóčhe has
become a refuge and home for many Indigenous nations
and peoples, including seven federally recognized Ojibwe
nations. We humbly encourage our readers to reflect upon
the historical legacies held in the lands they occupy.

milkweed.org

Milkweed Editions, an independent nonprofit publisher, gratefully acknowledges sustaining support from our Board of Directors; the Alan B. Slifka Foundation and its president, Riva Ariella Ritvo-Slifka; the Amazon Literary Partnership; the Ballard Spahr Foundation; *Copper Nickel*; the McKnight Foundation; the National Endowment for the Arts; the National Poetry Series; and other generous contributions from foundations, corporations, and individuals. Also, this activity is made possible by the voters of Minnesota through a Minnesota State Arts Board Operating Support grant, thanks to a legislative appropriation from the arts and cultural heritage fund. For a full listing of Milkweed Editions supporters, please visit milkweed.org.